MATT CAMERON is an award-winning playwright and screenwriter. His plays include *Tear from a Glass Eye*, winner of the Wal Cherry Play of the Year Award with productions by Playbox, Black Swan and the Gate Theatre in London, where he was nominated Most Promising Playwright in the Evening Standard Awards; *Footprints on Water*, winner of the British Council International New Playwriting Award with productions by Neonheart, Griffin and La Mama; *Mr Melancholy*, winner of the ANPC/New Dramatists Award with productions by Griffin, La Boite, Chameleon, New York Stage & Film in New York, Theatre de l'Erre in Paris and Teatr Ad Spectatores in Poland; and *The Eskimo Calling*, produced by Neonheart and Belvoir B Sharp. *Hinterland*, nominated for the NSW Premier's Literary Award; *Man the Balloon*, nominated for the Victorian Premier's Literary Award; and a short play *Whispering Death* were all produced by Melbourne Theatre Company. *Poor Boy*, featuring the songs of Tim Finn, was nominated for the Victorian Premier's Literary Award and co-produced by Melbourne and Sydney Theatre Companies. *Ruby Moon* was nominated for the Queensland Premier's Literary Award and has been produced by Playbox, Neonheart, Queensland Theatre Company, Melbourne Theatre Company, Sydney Theatre Company, State Theatre Company of South Australia, Northern Stage in England and Théâtre Claque in Switzerland. Screen credits include *Jack Irish*, *Seachange*, *Crashburn* and the AWGIE award-winning *Introducing Gary Petty*.

RUBY MOON

Matt Cameron

Currency Press, Sydney

CURRENCY PLAYS

First published in 2003
by Currency Press Pty Ltd,
PO Box 2287, Strawberry Hills, NSW, 2012, Australia
enquiries@currency.com.au
www.currency.com.au
Revised edition published 2005

Reprinted 2005, 2006, 2009, 2010, 2011, 2013, 2014, 2015, 2016, 2017, 2018,
2019, 2020, 2022

Cataloguing-in-Publication data for this title is available from the National
Library of Australia website: www.nla.gov.au
Set by Dean Nottle
Cover design by Mollison
Front cover image features Christen O'Leary

Contents

Currency Press acknowledges the Traditional Owners of the Country on which we live and work. We pay our respects to all Aboriginal and Torres Strait Islander Elders, past and present.

Introduction

Matt Cameron

In many ways the published play defies the essentially ephemeral nature of theatre. I happen to subscribe to the notion that a play is only ever truly finished when the playwright is dead. Hence, fortuitously, I have continued to tinker with the text of *Ruby Moon* and now, much to my pernickety relief, here is the new version developed courtesy of Aidan Fennessy's stunning production for Playbox and Neonheart. The originally published text contained, to my chagrin, several sequences which were removed or improved in rehearsals, previews and subsequent performances. However, despite these initial script flaws, I was extremely fortunate to have the play realised in its first incarnation by a talented team of artists collaborating at the peak of their considerable powers and I owe them all a debt of gratitude.

Ruby Moon is a story about a little girl who sets off to visit her grandma, just like a fairytale, but never arrives. The child randomly taken from our midst is an all-too-common tragedy which threatens us in a deeply primal way. Innocence is corrupted and our world is distorted, with even the benign rendered ominous. This play is acutely theatrical in its conceit and set in the fictional Flaming Tree Grove, a slice of David Lynch suburbia where a dark underbelly lurks beneath an idyllic, picture-perfect veneer.

I grew up in the suburbs of Melbourne among rows of anonymous and homogenous houses, a place precariously pleased with itself, a time of slow summer days etched with the echo of Mr Whippy's ice-cream van, of streets filled with children enchanted by the clarion call of 'Greensleeves'. Mr Whippy was suburbia's Pied Piper, crawling by in hypnotically sinister slow motion. Even if you didn't have coins in your pocket you'd run after him in the hope of a benevolent miracle. Mostly you ended up watching smug children lick their ice-creams. But even the watching was an event.

It was a world where neighbours dutifully waved but had no idea who each other really was or what went on over the fence, behind the curtains. For that is the ingenious deceit of suburbia: that proximity equals intimacy, fraternity, community. The suburbs can be a very lonely place, their great myth being that by huddling together we are inherently safe. But the darker recesses of human nature have never operated on a geographic principle.

Parents are now necessarily more vigilant and suspicious but my own childhood felt like the last of those trusting days of yore, when front doors were left unlocked, when the entire neighbourhood was your backyard. There was but one prevailing rule: be home when the street lights come on. And the instant we heard the tell-tale buzz of overhead lamps flickering into action the streets became a blur of children scurrying towards the warm glow of home. Sometimes after dark the neighbourhood would echo with the sound of parents' voices calling tardy children in for dinner. We would hear those calls and never for a moment think that the child might not be coming home.

The conception of *Ruby Moon* from the outset was for two actors to inhabit all of its eccentric characters. The chameleonic properties of the actor, transforming before our very eyes: for me it is the essence of theatre magic. Theatre exists in the imagination of the beholder. It is as much about the surrounding darkness as it is about the light. A solitary spotlight on an actor on an otherwise dark stage draws our eye to the character and the story they tell within that light, but it also makes us wonder about the darkness being pierced. What do we imagine exists in that darkness?

The theatre is, quite wonderfully, artifice. Its very lifeblood is the suspension of disbelief. It is about doors within false walls that seem real, that lead nowhere and yet everywhere, and behind them, beyond them, the world of our imagination, the backstage of our existence, vast realms of parallel life. To me the theatre has always seemed a beautiful lie.

All of which, I hope, is at play within this play.

> '… a blind man in a dark room looking for a black hat which isn't there.'
>
> (Lord Bowen)

For me this quote resonates with the mystery at the heart of *Ruby Moon*. It is not necessarily about the black hat. It is about the blind man in the dark room looking for it.

Melbourne
June, 2005

Ruby Moon was first produced by Playbox and Neonheart at the Malthouse Theatre, Melbourne, on 30 July 2003, with the following cast:

RAY, SID, SONNY JIM, CARL	Peter Houghton
SYLVIE, DULCIE, VERONICA, DAWN	Christen O'Leary

Director, Aidan Fennessy
Designer, Christina Smith
Lighting Designer, Philip Lethlean
Original Music, Andrew McNaughton

The author would like to especially thank Aidan Fennessy, Peter Houghton, Christen O'Leary, Neonheart Theatre and Playbox Theatre Company for assisting the development of the play.

CHARACTERS

SYLVIE MOON, the mother
RAY MOON, the father
DULCIE DOILY, the spinster
SID CRAVEN, the clown
VERONICA VALE, the singer
SONNY JIM, the soldier
DAWN BERGER, the babysitter
CARL OGLE, the inventor

The play is written for one male and one female actor to play all of the above roles.

There are also recorded voice-overs:

RUBY MOON
GRANDMA MOON
DETECTIVE HOLLOWAY

PLAYWRIGHT'S NOTE

Ruby Moon involves a theatrical conceit, with two actors playing all the characters in the play. They need not make wholesale changes in costume, hair and make-up. Rather they adjust simply and swiftly from the base attire worn by the characters of Ray and Sylvie and use props, coats and hats along with body, voice and perhaps accents to create each new character. The intention is that the play moves fluidly between scenes.

The play runs strictly without interval.

THE SETTING

A timeless, placeless world featuring an armchair, standing lamp, rocking horse, gramophone, telephone, answering machine and coat stand with various garments. The furnishings are antique in a room evoking dust-covered memory. Upstage is a blood-red velvet curtain and scrim, allowing objects to 'appear' and 'disappear' with light. There is also a street lamp and the bare branches of blackened trees pointing like gnarled fingers through a vivid night sky. A full moon hovers.

PROLOGUE

The sound of a distorted music-box version of 'Greensleeves' crackling from an ice-cream van speaker. SYLVIE *is in the armchair.* RAY *stands motionless. They stare absently as the rocking horse rocks slowly back and forth. The sound of distant thunder rumbling and rain falling. It fades. Ruby's ghostly whisper reverberates like a secret.*

RUBY: [*voice-over*] It begins like a fairytale…

> RAY *and* SYLVIE *are shaken from their reverie. He shakes his umbrella. She sits up.*

SYLVIE: What was that?

RAY: [*calling*] It's only me, baby. I'm home.

SYLVIE: Did you say something?

RAY: I said, 'I'm home'. Do I get a kiss?

SYLVIE: Sounds like it's coming down cats and dogs.

RAY: Yes, domestic pets are pelting from the sky.

SYLVIE: How was the world today?

RAY: Its usual self. It asks after you.

SYLVIE: Give it my best, won't you.

RAY: What news from the home front?

SYLVIE: All quiet. Not a peep. Look at you, Ray. You're soaked.

RAY: Is there anything more futile than holding up a broken umbrella in the rain?

She takes the umbrella and helps him remove his coat.

SYLVIE: You'll catch your death out there.

RAY: These nights are getting colder, I swear.

She hangs up the coat and umbrella.

Do I get a kiss?

He waits for a kiss that never comes.

SYLVIE: Busy at the store?

RAY: The train was full tonight.

SYLVIE: Wish this rain would stop.

RAY: Have you had your lie down?

SYLVIE: How do we do this again?

They stare at each other.

RAY: It was busy today.

SYLVIE: Well, it is a peak-hour train.

RAY: Still, it's good for the garden.

SYLVIE: I had a little rest this afternoon.

They stare at each other.

Yes, that's it.

RAY: Our friend Sid came into the store again.

SYLVIE: From number two?

RAY: He was bothering the customers. Reading the picture books aloud. I had a good mind to report him… Any messages?

He presses the button on the answering machine. The sound of Grandma Moon's voice.

GRANDMA MOON: [*voice-over*] It's only me. Has the little one left yet? [*Beep.*] Still no sign of her… [*Beep.*] Hello? Ray…? Ray?!

The sound of a final beep.

RAY: When are we going to erase those?

SYLVIE: Leave them.

Silence.

RAY: Sonny Jim's limp isn't getting any better. I passed him in the cemetery on the way home.

SYLVIE: Walking that nasty dog of his?

RAY: It was paying its respects on one of the graves again.

SYLVIE: As if death wasn't insult enough…

RAY: They still haven't cut the grass at number seven. It's an eyesore.
  Someone should have a word.
SYLVIE: I heard both parents were bed-ridden with no income to
  speak of.
RAY: They must miss Dawn's babysitting money.
SYLVIE: Bad things happen in houses like that.
RAY: They bring down the street.
SYLVIE: Such a pretty little street.
RAY: How about a kiss?
SYLVIE: Can you hear that?

> *Silence.*

RAY: You're imagining things.
SYLVIE: Listen…

> *Out of the silence a naïve piano refrain echoes. They listen.*

She's playing again… Can you hear her? That's not from the music
books. That's her own tune. She practises it for hours. Isn't she
clever…?

> *She listens intently.*

[*Singing*] 'She's not in the room
She's not outside
Hide from the world
The curtain girl…'

> *The music disappears.*

RAY: Where is that from?
SYLVIE: I told you. It's hers. She made it up.
RAY: She was only six.
SYLVIE: Past tense.
RAY: Somebody must have taught it to her, Sylvie. The words, the tune.
SYLVIE: She's been here before. I always said that, Ray. She's an old
  soul.
RAY: Always hiding behind the curtain. Wearing it like a dress.
SYLVIE: Little feet poking out underneath.
RAY: 'Where's Ruby? Where can she be hiding?'

> *He hangs his head. She looks out.*

SYLVIE: Did you see him hiding out there before?
RAY: The wizard?

SYLVIE: Behind the flame tree.

RAY: Has he been bothering you?

SYLVIE: He knocked this morning after you left for work.

RAY: You didn't answer it?

SYLVIE: I kept the curtains closed all day.

RAY: I thought I saw him loitering in front of the school...

The telephone rings. SYLVIE *stares at it.*

SYLVIE: Are you going to get that?

RAY *doesn't move. She picks it up.*

[*Into the phone*] Hello...? Hello, you. Where are you calling from...? Are you keeping out of this rain...? When are you coming home...?

RAY *stares at her.*

[*Into the phone*] We're not going anywhere... We'll be right here...

RAY: Who are you talking to?

SYLVIE: [*into the phone*] Yes, he's here.

RAY: Sylvie, who is it?

SYLVIE: [*lowering the phone from her ear*] It's her.

Silence. RAY *takes the phone.*

RAY: [*into the phone*] Hello...? Hello...? Hello...?

He slowly hangs up.

SYLVIE: I heard it ring.

RAY: Sounds like that rain's easing.

SYLVIE: Didn't you hear it ring?

RAY: Why don't you give us a kiss?

SYLVIE: She must be soaked to the bone.

RAY: Sylvie...?

SYLVIE: Did you leave the key under the mat for her?

RAY: What happened? Why are you in such a state?

SYLVIE: I'm always in a state! Don't you know, Ray? I haven't been well.

RAY *offers her a glass of water and a bottle of pills. She feigns swallowing one of the pills and pockets it when he is not looking.*

RAY: I could read you the story, baby?

SYLVIE: Yes, tell me the story, Ray. I want to hear the story.

She fetches a worn leather book. They sit on the armchair.

With the voices. Do the different voices.
RAY: [*reading*] 'It had been one of those scorching summer days
When all the world appears ablaze
Sprinklers swivelled to a hypnotic beat
Cicadas pulsed to the shimmering heat
Concrete was caramel under your feet and
The ice-cream van turned slow motion into the dead-end street.
    She turns the page.
The setting sun lit the flame trees one by one
Her mother looked down the grove like the barrel of a gun
As the little girl turned like a page to wave farewell
Before skipping away down the path to hell.'
    He snaps the book shut.
SYLVIE: Don't stop. Keep going.
RAY: I can't do the story tonight.
SYLVIE: You have to.
RAY: I can't bear it.
    He gets up and slams the book down.
SYLVIE: I want to know how it ends.
RAY: It doesn't end well.
SYLVIE: I don't want to hear that story.
RAY: [*shaking her fiercely*] Grow up, Sylvie! Grow up!
    He releases her. Silence.
SYLVIE: Can I have the book?
    He hands her the book.
    She loves her stories, Ray. She'll never be too old for them.
RAY: Every night they were new again.
SYLVIE: Past tense.
RAY: Knew them by heart. If you missed a word she pounced on it.
SYLVIE: Past tense!
RAY: I'll get you your cup of tea.
SYLVIE: Stop speaking in past tense!
RAY: Shush, baby, the neighbours.
SYLVIE: Haven't you seen them looking sideways at us, Ray? Keeping a
    safe distance? They used to leave soup on our doorstep… flowers…
RAY: Maybe our grief has reached its use-by date…

SYLVIE: They all wish we'd move.

RAY: We don't know that.

SYLVIE: Tell me what we know, Ray.

RAY: Not tonight, Sylvie.

SYLVIE: It helps when you tell me what we know.

> *Silence.*

RAY: We know she set off to visit her grandma but never arrived.

SYLVIE: We know her butterfly clip was found in the gutter outside Veronica Vale in number five.

RAY: Beside an upturned, melted ice-cream.

SYLVIE: The cracked cone rising up from the bitumen.

RAY: Like the Wicked Witch of the West's crooked hat.

SYLVIE: But she didn't have money to buy an ice-cream.

RAY: We don't know that.

SYLVIE: We know Miss Doily from next door's parrot was up in the flame tree out front.

RAY: 'Who's a pretty girl?'

SYLVIE: 'Who's a pretty girl…?' I watched her set off into the dying sun, when the world is askew, and I know how this sounds, Ray, but I distinctly heard the parrot say, 'Where's the pretty girl?'

RAY: We don't know that.

SYLVIE: 'Where's the pretty girl…?' Like a prophecy. That was when I heard the phone ring. Which surprised me because the repairman's van was still parked out front of Professor Ogle's place. Remember the heat had short-circuited the wires? It was six forty-eight. When your train gets in. And I hurried inside. I knew it was you calling from the station.

RAY: Like I always do.

SYLVIE: It was our ritual.

RAY: Past tense.

SYLVIE: Twelve minutes walk away.

RAY: Through the back of the church and down the laneway next to number five.

SYLVIE: Dinner on the table at seven.

RAY: But it wasn't on the table.

SYLVIE: I had to race in to tell Dulcie Doily about her escaped parrot up in the tree. She was very agitated. 'Your little devil needs her mouth washed out.' I told her my daughter was not—

RAY: Past tense.

SYLVIE: … is not the kind of girl to curse. By the time I got back you were here on the phone eating an ice-cream.

RAY: I felt like a treat.

SYLVIE: 'You'll spoil your dinner', I said.

RAY: There was no dinner.

Silence.

SYLVIE: What else do we know?

RAY: We know I was on the phone to Grandma Moon. She was concerned because Ruby hadn't arrived. She'd left those messages.

SYLVIE: We know we searched the street. One side each. Knocking on every door.

RAY: We know we called the police. Missing persons.

SYLVIE: With their list that goes on forever. We must pass missing people every day.

RAY: We know the case remains officially open.

SYLVIE: We know we stopped hearing from Detective Holloway.

RAY: 'You need to prepare for the worst.' How does anyone do that…?

SYLVIE: There's always something worse than the worst you can imagine…

RAY: But you never know…

SYLVIE: We didn't bury her, so…

RAY: You never know.

SYLVIE: She was probably taken and… hurt. We have to accept that. That she was hurt. By someone.

RAY: It's been too long.

Silence. She fetches a small, brown paper package.

SYLVIE: So why after all this time would someone send this?

She hands it to RAY.

It was in the letterbox…

He opens the lid and slowly removes a plastic doll's arm.

RAY: What am I to make of this, Sylvie?

SYLVIE: It's Ruby Doll's arm.

RAY: We don't know that.

SYLVIE: We do.

RAY: You can't just give this to me with no warning.

SYLVIE: We both know exactly what this is, Ray. It won't be ignored.
RAY: [*examining the package*] No postmark.
SYLVIE: No handwriting.
RAY: Did she have the doll with her that day?
SYLVIE: I don't know.
RAY: How can you not know? It's a lead. A clue. The detective's case may depend on it.
SYLVIE: Why didn't you think to ask until now?
RAY: Have you checked her room? Is the doll in her room?
SYLVIE: [*shaking her head*] She must have had it with her. Someone's trying to tell us something.
RAY: It could be from Ruby Doll…
SYLVIE: She did love that doll.
RAY: Past tense.
SYLVIE: Remember she came home with it the week before?
RAY: The doll dressed up exactly like her.
SYLVIE: We kept asking, 'Who gave you the doll, baby?'
RAY: She said she'd promised not to tell.
SYLVIE: We thought maybe Grandma Moon.
RAY: She swore it wasn't her.
SYLVIE: But her memory was going.
RAY: We should have found out who gave her that doll.
SYLVIE: We didn't know it mattered until now.

    Silence. She stares at the package.

Ray…? What if this is what he's doing to her? What if he's… dismantling our little girl?
RAY: We mustn't jump to conclusions.
SYLVIE: This changes everything.
RAY: Maybe it's a prank.
SYLVIE: This is a message.
RAY: If we just knew who gave it to her. That might give us something.
SYLVIE: [*looking out*] What if it was one of them…? We could ask.
RAY: We can't knock on their doors again, Sylvie. They'll think we're mad.
SYLVIE: We have to. One side each. Just like that first night.

SCENE ONE

A solitary spotlight on RAY. *He walks on the spot to the sounds of the street at night: a chill wind, a distant barking dog and a wind chime. He stops still. The sound of a door chime playing the tune: 'Kum Bah Yah'.*

DULCIE: Come in, come in...

An elderly spinster, DULCIE, *adjusts her apron and carries in a covered birdcage.* RAY *takes in the room.*

I just put her down for the night.

RAY: Sorry to be calling this late.

DULCIE: I keep late hours. Often pop down to the church to practise the organ. Just sang her my favourite hymn. Always sends her off to sleep.

RAY: I can imagine... What's it called?

DULCIE: 'Kum Bah Yah'.

RAY: The parrot?

DULCIE: Her name's Polly.

RAY: Oh, unusual...

DULCIE: My little gift from God.

She peers into the cage and does a parrot's voice between barely-moving lips. Initially this is disguised, but the charade becomes apparent and is done without acknowledgement.

[*As the parrot*] Aark, hallelujah. [*As herself*] Yes, Polly, hallelujah. [*As the parrot*] Aark, hallelujah. [*As herself*] Yes, shush now. Go to sleep.

She leaves the cage and returns to RAY.

I think that's done it. Thank the Lord. [*As the parrot*] Aark, hallelujah.

RAY *realises that* DULCIE *is doing the parrot's voice. She has stopped turning away to disguise it.*

[*As herself*] Yes, Polly. Nigh-night. I have to be careful not to say L-o-r-d or G-o-d or she'll never drop off. [*As the parrot*] Aark, hallelujah.

Silence.

RAY: You don't suppose the bird can spell, Miss Doily?

DULCIE: Please Raymond, call me Dulcie. How is that poor wife of yours?

RAY: Much better.

DULCIE: Fragile creature. She must be a burden.

RAY: Getting stronger by the day.

DULCIE: I don't know how she can bear the guilt.

RAY: Why do you say that?

DULCIE: I'm not a mother but one does fear for the little lambs left alone to stray. And when one considers certain elements in the neighbourhood. Types like Mr Craven across the way. G-o-d only knows what goes on in that house.

RAY: She was visiting her grandma.

DULCIE: Just like the story. What was it? You'll know, you're in books. Was it the one with the wolf?

RAY: It's not like we sent her off into the dark woods, Dulcie. Ruby often walked down to her grandma's. She only lived at the end of the cul-de-sac.

DULCIE: And now she's dead.

RAY: We don't know that.

DULCIE: Grandma Moon.

RAY: Oh, yes.

DULCIE: Dear old thing. Blind as a bat. Deaf as a post. She could murder a hymn. Used to sit beside me in church. [*As the parrot*] Aark, peace be with you. [*As herself*] And also with you. Shush now. She's still learning. Very keen. I lost my last Polly. G-o-d rest her soul.

RAY: Dulcie, do you remember Ruby's doll? The one that looked like her?

DULCIE: I do vaguely recall a doll.

RAY: Did she have it with her that day? To go to her grandma's?

DULCIE: I wasn't in my right mind that day. Polly had gone missing.

RAY: Did Ruby ever tell you who gave her that doll?

DULCIE: She used to pretend it could talk. Which I found a little creepy. Do you keep a Bible in the home, Raymond?

RAY: Did she ever say where the doll came from, Miss Doily?

DULCIE: Dulcie, please. Every good home has a Bible. Without a moral compass a child is easily lost. Suffice to say, Ruby seemed unfamiliar with the scriptures. I still have her on our prayer list. And I drop the odd psalm in your letterbox to comfort Sylvie.

RAY: Did you happen to see anyone near our letterbox today?

DULCIE: She's in a better place now, Raymond. Out of harm's way.

Seated beside the Lord. [*As the parrot*] Aark, praise the Lord. [*As herself*] Hasn't missed a single Sunday service. Perches on my shoulder. Takes communion.

RAY: She's not with the Lord.

DULCIE: Don't listen to him, Polly.

RAY: What sort of God would take an innocent little girl?

DULCIE: Are you sure she was innocent?

Silence.

RAY: Dulcie, we think a piece of the puzzle may have been overlooked. We think that piece is her doll.

DULCIE: Raymond, you can't keep doing this to yourselves. She's not coming back.

RAY: What about the Gallows boy?

DULCIE: That was a long time ago.

RAY: He came back.

DULCIE: But he was never quite right. To say nothing of his... [*She gestures to her face.*] Well, you know, the mask...

RAY: Has anyone ever seen his face?

DULCIE: I shudder to think. I hear he's horribly disfigured. Something unspeakable happened to that boy. One does pity the poor wretch but one must keep one's distance from types like that. Does he still knock on your door?

RAY: [*nodding*] Mostly he just watches from under the street lamp.

DULCIE: Says he's a wizard, you know. Black magic. The devil's work.

RAY: Taken from his bed, they said. In the dead of night. Just disappeared off the face of the earth.

DULCIE: The Lord giveth and he taketh away. [*As the parrot*] Aark, hallelujah. [*As herself*] To come back all those years later. All grown-up.

RAY: To knock on our door.

DULCIE: Only to find his parents had sold up. Moved on. Given up the ghost.

RAY: Who could blame them?

DULCIE: You have to let go too, Raymond. There is evil in this world.

RAY: Did you give Ruby the doll, Dulcie?

DULCIE: I most certainly did not. And I'll have you know you have no right to keep coming in here accusing a sweet, old lady.

RAY: This will be the last time.

DULCIE: You say that but it never is. Why can't you just accept that the man upstairs had his reasons?

RAY: We're not church-going people, Miss Doily.

Silence.

DULCIE: Let me tell you about your little angel, Mr Moon. It's no secret that my previous Polly lost her way that fateful day. Out of nowhere I was confronted with a blaspheming parrot. One could scarcely believe the foul language that came out of that beak. I taught her to say, 'Who's a pretty girl?', 'Polly want a cracker', as well as select Christian blessings. It's only me here so it's nice to have someone to talk to. But after leaving her alone with your Ruby that day it was as if she was suddenly possessed. And it can only have been the strength of the Devil himself who forced open that cage door. [*She looks out.*] How long are you going to leave her out there?

RAY: As long as it takes.

DULCIE: Detective Holloway was of the opinion that it no longer serves a purpose. Indeed, one might find it a touch morbid seeing her there by the kerb day after day, night after night.

RAY: Were you making a complaint?

DULCIE: It can't be helping either of you.

RAY: I was about to bring her in.

DULCIE: I think it's best. Time to move on.

RAY: Just to get her out of the rain. Get some dry clothes on.

DULCIE: Did you allow your child to play with Mr Craven from across the way?

RAY: Ruby never had anything to do with Sid Craven.

DULCIE: How strange. I saw her come out of there that day. I was putting seed out to lure Polly. She was jingling coins in her hand and went skipping off after the ice-cream van.

RAY *absorbs this as* DULCIE *sits with her Bible.*

[*Singing to herself*] 'Kum bah yah, my Lord… Kum bah yah…'

RAY: Don't get up, Miss Doily. I'll see myself out.

DULCIE: How does that story end, Raymond? With the little girl and the wolf? Does it end well?

RAY: The woodsman saves her with his axe.

DULCIE: Hmm, that's some comfort. Mind you, she wasn't missing this long. And she was a good little girl. Taking food to her sick grandma. Not one to curse. Yes, the Lord looked out for her.

RAY *tries to peer under the cover of the cage but is startled by* DULCIE.

[*As the parrot*] Aark, bugger the Lord. Bugger the Lord. [*As herself*] Shush now, Polly…

RAY: Goodnight…

DULCIE *smiles sweetly at* RAY.

DULCIE: [*as the parrot*] Aark, where's the pretty girl…?

She picks up the cage and retreats, staring at RAY.

[*As the parrot*] Aark, where's the pretty girl…?

SCENE TWO

The naïve piano refrain echoes. RAY *carries in the Ruby mannequin. It is dressed in a ruby-red dress with white dots and red shoes. The hair is bedraggled and the face smeared with red lipstick and rosy cheeks.* SYLVIE *appears.*

SYLVIE: Oh, baby! Look at you! You're soaked. Let's get you out of those wet things. Get a towel, Ray!

She peels off the dress. RAY *fetches a towel.*

You're shivering… It's okay, you're safe now… Mummy's here… Who did this to your face, baby?

RAY *hands over the towel.* SYLVIE *dries the mannequin and wipes the face clean.*

RAY: You're not getting better.

SYLVIE: Will you fetch me another dress.

RAY: It's not her, Sylvie. You know that.

SYLVIE: Let me pretend.

RAY: That's all we do.

SYLVIE: Feel her, Ray. She's chilled to the bone.

RAY *doesn't move.*

Fetch me another dress.

RAY: Which one?

SYLVIE: You know which one.

She dries the mannequin.

Is that better, baby? Hmm?

RAY: I don't know where they are, Sylvie.

SYLVIE: Oh, I'll get it.

RAY *is left alone with the mannequin. He suddenly pulls the arm off and stares at it.* SYLVIE *returns with a clean replica dress, to see* RAY *holding the arm.*

What have you done?!

RAY: Nothing. It fell off. It's okay, baby.

He re-attaches the arm. SYLVIE *dresses the mannequin.*

SYLVIE: Help me, Ray... help me put it on.

He helps put on the dress.

RAY: This has to stop.

SYLVIE: What did Dulcie say?

RAY: I'm sure you can imagine.

SYLVIE: I want to hear it from you.

RAY: The woman is quite mad.

SYLVIE: What did she say?

RAY: Same as always. 'The Lord took her.' And she wants us to stop leaving the mannequin at the kerb.

SYLVIE: Don't call her that.

RAY: She complained to the detective. She says Sid Craven gave Ruby the money for the ice-cream... Do we trust him?

SYLVIE: Do we trust her?

They stare at the mannequin.

RAY: Let me put her under the house tonight. Then I'll take her back to the store tomorrow.

SYLVIE: Look at that face, Ray. They can't put that in a display window. She's ours now. And she's going back out on the kerb. For everyone to see.

RAY: But they know what she looked like, baby.

SYLVIE: Past tense.

RAY: It's not helping. It hasn't led to any reports. Maybe it's time we...?

SYLVIE: 'Moved on'? Ray, there's nowhere from here. Let them look at her. Day and night. Through the cracks in their curtains. Let them see what was stolen from us.

They form a family portrait behind the mannequin as they stare out.

SCENE THREE

A solitary spotlight on SYLVIE. *She walks on the spot to the sounds of the street at night: whistling wind, wind chime and a distant wooden pipe playing the naïve refrain.* SID *laughs.*

SID: [*calling*] Is that you?

> *He pulls a cord to switch on the lamp he is hiding behind. He wears a grimy, blood-stained singlet under his suspenders. He also wears a skull cap, as worn under a wig.*

SYLVIE: The door was open, Sid. I hope you don't mind.

SID: Please, call me Sid.

SYLVIE: I did.

> SID *pulls the cord to switch off the lamp. He laughs.*

I can't see you there.

SID: Um… I'm not here.

SYLVIE: Is something the matter, Sid?

> SID *pulls the cord to switch on the lamp.*

Where did that blood come from?

SID: I don't want you to see me like this.

SYLVIE: Ray says he saw you in at the store today?

SID: Um… I wasn't there.

> *He pulls the cord to switch off the lamp.*

SYLVIE: Why don't you leave the light on, Sid? I feel better with it on.

SID: Are you afraid of me, Mrs Moon?

SYLVIE: Why? Should I be?

> SID *pulls the cord to switch on the lamp.*

SID: I don't mean any harm.

SYLVIE: I've never seen you without your face on. Remember I used to pass you in town when I was putting up posters? Do you still imitate strangers?

> *He imitates* SYLVIE*'s voice and gestures.*

SID: Do you still imitate strangers?
SYLVIE: You should keep your door locked. It's not safe out.
SID: Um, um, um… 'Doors are locked. Windows shut tight. Curtains drawn on this once-friendly picture-book neighbourhood.'
SYLVIE: Who said that?

He continues to imitate SYLVIE.

SID: Who said that?
SYLVIE: Please don't copy me.
SID: Please don't copy me.
SYLVIE: Sid, stop it!
SID: Are you going to hurt me?
SYLVIE: People don't like you doing that.

Silence.

Why would you think I'd hurt you?
SID: Why else would you be here?
SYLVIE: I'm seeing everyone on this side of the street. Have you done something wrong?

SID *shrugs.*

Whose blood is that?
SID: I didn't do anything. They just kept hitting.

He demonstrates a violent beating.

SYLVIE: Who?
SID: People don't like clowns anymore.

He winces as he takes a step and removes his shoe to empty a small stone into his hat.

SYLVIE: You can never trust a stranger, Sid. And you should always lock your door.
SID: No one comes in here.
SYLVIE: Miss Doily says Ruby came in here.
SID: I leave the door open for her. But she doesn't visit anymore.

He puts his shoe back on and winces.

SYLVIE: So she did visit?
SID: I made her face.

He takes off his shoe to empty another small stone. He continues to tap the shoe and an absurdly steady stream of stones cascade out into his hat. SYLVIE *watches.*

SYLVIE: And did you give her the doll?

SID: Little Ruby?

SYLVIE: Did you give her Little Ruby to play with?

SID: She played with me.

He taps out the last stone and puts on his shoe.

I feel bad about Ruby.

SYLVIE: Why do you say that, Sid?

SID: I miss her.

SYLVIE: It's not like you're responsible.

SID: Um, um, um… 'In many ways perhaps we all are. All of us in our most secret selves, in our darkest hour, are capable of what is unconscionable.'

SYLVIE: I need you to be serious, Sid.

SID adopts an exaggeratedly serious pose.

I need you to recall that day.

SID slips into a routine. He adopts the pose of a distraught mother searching. His voices are cartoon-like.

SID: [*calling, as Sylvie*] 'Ruby…? Ruby…? Where are you…?'

He adopts the pose of a stoic but worried father.

[*As Ray*] 'Ruby…? Ruby…?'

He makes the sound of a police car siren approaching and pulling up, followed by the car door opening and closing. He mimics the sound of the police car radio.

[*As a distorted radio voice*] 'VKC to BKV, come in, over…'

He plays a detective. He knocks on an imaginary door, makes the sound of it creaking open, holds up a 'badge' and writes in a 'notebook' as he chews 'gum'.

[*As the detective*] 'Blah blah blah blah blah blah, Senior Detective, blah blah blah.'

He slips into playing a police dog. He sniffs and barks before becoming a search party officer issuing muffled instructions through a megaphone.

[*As the officer*] 'Please remain in your homes. Do not, I repeat, do not come out into the street.'

He is blinded by flash 'photographs'.

[*As Sylvie*] 'If anyone knows where my baby is, please come forward.'
He 'sobs'. He shields his eyes from more flash 'photographs'.
[*As Ray*] 'We just want our little girl home safe.'
He plays a horde of hungry journalists and photographers.
'One more! Mr Moon! Mrs Moon! Over here! This way!'
He plays a television reporter delivering his report.
'According to police sources, foul play is suspected and child welfare groups are already calling on parents not to encourage children to kiss adults goodbye as it may make them vulnerable to predatory advances.'
He makes a thumping knock on an imaginary door, followed by the sound of it creaking open. He chews 'gum' and holds up the 'badge'.
[*As the detective*] 'Sid Craven, can you account for your whereabouts at six forty-eight p.m.?' [*As himself*] 'Um… I was playing with Ruby.'
[*As the detective*] 'Cuff him, boys. Let's get this clown down to the station.'
He pretends he is handcuffed and being dragged away.
[*As himself*] 'I shouldn't be out this late.'
He sits down and plays a victim tied to a chair, looking up fearfully at his interrogator. He stands to play the detective, who menacingly stubs out his 'cigarette'.
[*As the detective*] 'Blah blah blah blah blah blah… Pervert!'
He sits down to play the victim tied to the chair.
[*As himself*] 'I don't understand!'
He stands to play the interrogating detective.
[*As the detective*] 'What rock did you crawl out from, you sick freak?'
He sits down to play the victim tied to the chair.
[*As himself*] 'I didn't hurt her!'
He makes the sound of punches and his head swings from side to side with the 'blows'.
'I swear I didn't do it!'
More 'blows' as he is tortured mercilessly.

'She's my friend!'

He sobs, genuinely. He slowly gets up and approaches SYLVIE.
*He holds out his upturned hat. She drops in some coins. He
immediately stops crying.*

SYLVIE: Why didn't they arrest you?

SID: Um… no proof.

SYLVIE: Did you buy Ruby the ice-cream, Sid? Dulcie says Ruby came
out of your house jingling coins in her hand.

Silence.

SID: What are you going to do me?

SYLVIE: Were you in the habit of giving my daughter treats?

SID: I didn't hurt her.

SYLVIE: Did she bring you back an ice-cream?

SID: She was bringing back my photo.

SYLVIE: What photo?

SID: Veronica Vale at number five. Ruby was friendly with her. She was
going to get her to autograph my photo.

SYLVIE: You must be mistaken, Sid. Our family has no acquaintance
with Ms Vale.

SID: She was always in there.

SYLVIE: What were you doing spying on my child?

SID: I wasn't. I was spying on Veronica. Have you heard her? It's like
listening to velvet.

He slips into playing a chanteuse.

[*Singing, as Veronica*] 'The crying bed…' Um… 'Take back those
words unsaid…'

SYLVIE: She sings?

SID: You should see her at night. When she comes out to play. The
curtains part and she puts on a show.

SYLVIE: What was she doing with Ruby?

SID: It was secret.

SYLVIE: What happened to that photograph?

SID: That's just it. She never came back. I lost my photo.

SYLVIE: I lost my baby girl.

Silence.

Sid, do you know where she is?

SID: Um… it's not safe out. They hurt you for no reason. They crush you because they can. They hate beauty.

SYLVIE: Did she have the doll when you last saw her?

> SID *nods.*

And you haven't sent us a package? You haven't been near our letterbox?

> *He shakes his head.*

What did you two do in here together?

SID: She played with me.

SYLVIE: She was your 'friend', you say?

SID: I don't have friends now. But I'm a friendly person.

> *He looks out.*

SYLVIE: What time does her curtain come up?

SID: She keeps you guessing.

SYLVIE: It's already late…

SID: When the stars come out to shine…

> *He takes up his vigil.*

SYLVIE: You like Veronica, don't you, Sid?

SID: Yes, thank you. Very much.

SYLVIE: Do you imagine her being your friend?

SID: Um… it's not like that.

SYLVIE: Sid… I know it's you.

> *Silence.*

Stay away from my mannequin.

SID: I didn't do anything.

SYLVIE: We never let Ruby wear make-up. She was too young.

SID: But she liked me making her face disappear.

SYLVIE: Don't go near her again.

> *The Ruby mannequin stands under the street lamp with the moon hovering.*

SCENE FOUR

An ominous knock at the door echoes. SYLVIE *listens anxiously to it in the dim light.*

SYLVIE: [*whispering*] Ray...? Do you hear that? It's him again.
RAY: Just ignore it.

> *They listen in silence.*

SYLVIE: He has no right to keep doing this.
RAY: He's harmless enough.
SYLVIE: We don't know that.

> *Another slow knock at the door echoes.*

The man calls himself a wizard, Ray. He stands out there staring at our house. Knocking on our door at all hours.
RAY: We have nothing to fear from Mr Gallows, baby. If anything, he's our beacon of hope. He came back.
SYLVIE: There's a dark heart beating in that man...

> *They listen in silence.*

RAY: There. Sounds like he's gone.

> *He turns on the lamp.*

Shall I sneak a peek to set your mind at ease?
SYLVIE: If he sees you he'll only keep knocking.
RAY: I'll send him on his way and then check under the house.
SYLVIE: Dulcie says she saw him once inside Grandma Moon's.
RAY: I'm sure she was mistaken.
SYLVIE: He was at the sink in the kitchen in broad daylight. She said she had a clear view from the vestry window.
RAY: I check the locks regularly, Sylvie.
SYLVIE: Why won't you just sell it? Be done with the place.
RAY: It's not for sale.

> *Silence, then the sound of the naïve refrain played on a wooden pipe.*

SYLVIE: Ray... do you hear that? It's the tune. He's playing her tune on his pipe.

RAY: Perhaps he taught it to her?

They listen until the sound disappears.

SYLVIE: He used to play it for the children, lurking on the other side of the wall at the school. I remember now. And when they heard it they were all drawn to him. Like magic.

RAY: Mr Gallows is no magician, baby.

SYLVIE: He used to tell Ruby he could make things disappear.

RAY: Why don't you go back to work at the school, Sylvie? Get yourself out of the house? They miss you at the library and you used to love the little ones gathered round, wide-eyed, hanging on every word…

SYLVIE: No, Ray! I couldn't bear it…

A sharp knock at the door echoes. They are rattled.

Make him stop.

RAY: It might not be him, baby. What if it's one of the neighbours? What if it's the detective?

SYLVIE: He doesn't come here anymore.

RAY: What if it's her…?

SYLVIE: She could be trying to get in. Let her in.

RAY *leaves. The distorted sound of Ruby giggling.*

[*Whispering*] Ruby…? Baby…?

RAY *returns with a brown paper package.*

RAY: It was on the doorstep.

SYLVIE: Did you see him?

He shakes his head.

It must be him, Ray.

RAY: He's an old man. He can't move that fast.

SYLVIE: He's a wizard. He spirited her away into the night, playing his magic pipe.

RAY: We don't know that.

Silence.

SYLVIE: We should have confiscated that doll.

RAY: It would only have upset her.

SYLVIE: We should never have allowed it into the house. Someone gave it to gain her trust. They were grooming her. And we let them.

RAY: We don't have to open it.

They stare at the package.

Remember when we'd bring her home late at night...? After visiting friends...?

SYLVIE: 'Visiting friends'... It's a lifetime ago...

RAY: And she'd be all limp and sleepy in the back seat of the car. And I knew she wanted to be carried inside. Tucked tight in her cosy bed. Music-box ballerina doing her pirouette... I imagine them finding her like that. All limp and sleepy. Waiting for me to carry her safely inside.

SYLVIE: If she's not alive then she's only bones.

RAY: We don't know that.

> SYLVIE *opens the lid and holds up a doll's leg.* RAY *reaches in to remove the other doll's leg.*

SYLVIE: We're living the wrong lives, Ray. There must have been a mistake. These are other people's lives.

RAY: He'll slip up, baby. He's feeling safe. The newspapers have moved on. The grief tourists have come and gone. Parents are letting their children stray out of sight again. This is when we get him.

SYLVIE: Or her.

> RAY *closes the lid on the package.*

RAY: I think I'll take my walk.

SYLVIE: Must be closing in on show time?

RAY: I'm afraid you've lost me...

SYLVIE: Veronica Vale. She does a striptease in front of her window every night.

RAY: First I've heard.

SYLVIE: Wonder if all the men in Flaming Tree Grove watch her.

RAY: What is this street coming to...?

SYLVIE: She is the next house on your side.

RAY: If the light's on, I'll call by. See what I can find.

SYLVIE: I'll try number four.

SCENE FIVE

A solitary spotlight on RAY. *He pulls up his collar to brace against the cold as he peers through the window into Veronica's boudoir.*

RAY: [*whispering*] Behind the velvet curtain, the siren of the night, with the sweet caress of secrets confessed…

> VERONICA *is revealed wearing a wig, high heels, a lacy slip, a silk gown and a red feather boa. She blows dust off a record before placing it on the gramophone. The sound of the needle on a scratchy album.*

Flaming Tree Grove's midnight chanteuse…

> VERONICA *picks up an old microphone. Suddenly she is in a spotlight singing a torch song.*

VERONICA: [*singing*] 'All-too-familiar strangers rue stolen belief
Doubt creeps about like a pantomime thief
And you've gone to water

The crying bed
Take back those words unsaid
Drowned lovers found
In a crying bed

Into the sun
You run
And slowly set
And yet
Morning hides
From prisoners
Of the night
Guarded by regret

The crying bed
Take back those words unsaid
Drowned lovers found
In a crying bed

The crying bed
Another long night ahead

Drowned lovers found
Hold each other down
Washed up on old ground
Bound to our crying bed.'

> *She finishes with a flourish. The music ends. The sound of the record spinning under the needle. The spotlight disappears.* RAY *steps out of the shadows.*

Do you like my voice?

RAY: It's beautiful.

VERONICA: Sweet of you to say.

RAY: Should we draw the curtain, Veronica?

VERONICA: Let them watch.

> *She takes a drink from a small medicine bottle.*

Look at you... All shy. [*Holding up a watch*] You left this here last time, lover boy.

RAY: That's not my watch.

VERONICA: Oh, I see. We're playing this again, are we? You do love your little games.

> *She sashays over and offers her hand.*

Hello. Ray from number one, isn't it?

RAY: [*shaking her hand*] That's right.

VERONICA: [*pulling him close*] Come for another cup of sugar, Ray?

RAY: I've come about Ruby.

VERONICA: Surprise, surprise.

> *She removes the wig and takes another drink from the bottle, noting his disapproval.*

It soothes my throat.

RAY: Isn't it addictive?

VERONICA: Isn't everything?

> *She playfully slaps his behind. He is startled.*

You keep your wife medicated, don't you?

RAY: She hasn't been well.

VERONICA: She was never well. I saw her go into Sid's before.

RAY: Are you going to close the curtain?

VERONICA: What's to see? Just two neighbours talking.

RAY: Should we turn off the light?

VERONICA: Do you think she's watching us?

She looks out.

RAY: Sid says you knew Ruby.

VERONICA: We had an arrangement. She fetched my medicine from the chemist. They know me down there.

RAY: In return for what?

VERONICA *sings the naïve piano melody.*

VERONICA: [*singing as an off-key Ruby*] 'La la la la la...'

She blocks her ears and shudders at the memory.

RAY: You should have told us she was in here.

VERONICA: Why?

RAY: We're her parents.

VERONICA: I assumed you knew where she was.

RAY: Well, we...

VERONICA: I only gave her singing lessons, sugar. She preferred the company of grown-ups. Wanted to be a singer like yours truly. Wanted to be famous. And now she is. But I was never famous... I was notorious. [*She moves closer.*] My allure is founded entirely on dim lighting. I am nothing without the night.

He retreats.

Yes, why don't you run along home, Ray. No doubt your wife is waiting for you to come to bed.

RAY: She sleeps in Ruby's room. Has ever since. Not that either of us really sleeps. We did that first night. The police told us we'd need our strength. The sun was up when we woke and for a fleeting moment we listened for the sound of her practising the piano before breakfast, like always, but... What sort of parents could fall asleep?

VERONICA *drinks from her bottle.*

VERONICA: She did have a sweet little voice, I suppose.

RAY: I never heard her sing.

VERONICA: All that untouched youth...

RAY: We don't know that.

VERONICA: Truth is, I can't bear little girls. They don't know how the world works. I told her as much. How I loathe innocence. The innocent get what they deserve.

RAY: What do you think she deserved?

VERONICA: If you walk down the street in a little red dress you're playing with fire.

RAY: She was only a child.

VERONICA: Then take solace from that, Ray. This way she's preserved in all her arrested glory. Before being sullied by clawing men. Before all the misbegotten lust visited on the rest of us.

RAY: What if it's the last thing she ever knew?

> *Silence.*

You did take care of my little girl, didn't you?

> VERONICA *moves close to* RAY.

VERONICA: What do you say, Ray? Once more with feeling? Pressed up against the window. For all to see.

RAY: I think you've got the wrong idea…

> VERONICA *kisses* RAY, *slow and lingering. He responds and she pulls away, laughing at him.*

Please, Veronica, don't.

VERONICA: Who's a naughty boy?

RAY: Did she come here that day?

VERONICA: Are we still on this?

RAY: It's the reason I'm here.

VERONICA: Is it?

RAY: Answer me.

VERONICA: Are you accusing me of something?

RAY: I'm just trying to get things clear in my head.

VERONICA: Let it lie, Ray. Let it lie.

RAY: Sid says he gave her a photo of you to sign.

VERONICA: Sid! Believe me, he's not all there.

RAY: He's just a bit of a character. The street's full of them.

VERONICA: Doesn't mean you should trust them.

RAY: I don't.

VERONICA: Including me?

> *They stare at each other.*

RAY: I just want this to be over.

VERONICA: Do you?

> *Silence.*

I watch you parading your exquisite sadness, Ray. Riveted to your tragedy. But you don't have a patent on grief. You didn't invent pain.

RAY: Did you sign the photo, Veronica? The one Ruby was sent over here with?

VERONICA: And if I did, where would that leave you?

RAY: One step closer.

VERONICA: But you're walking on the spot, Ray. She must be a million miles away by now.

RAY: Did she make it to your door?

VERONICA: What do you think, lover boy?

RAY: I'm not your lover boy.

VERONICA: Don't you want to have your way with me?

RAY: When did you last see her?

VERONICA: Alive?

RAY: What do you—?

VERONICA: Or do you mean the last time?

RAY: Yes, but—

VERONICA: You know the soldier across the way?

RAY: Sonny Jim?

VERONICA: It may have been nothing. I can't be sure it was her.

RAY: Tell me!

VERONICA: He and his dog were digging in the church late at night. I saw Sonny Jim crouch over the hole with a wrapped bundle in his hands… It was some time after…

She slinks away.

But you never know…

SCENE SIX

SYLVIE *takes a deep breath at the door to number four. The harsh sound of a brass door-knocker.*

SONNY JIM: [*calling*] Who's there?

SYLVIE: [*calling*] It's Mrs Moon. Sylvie. From across the road.

A light switches on to reveal SONNY JIM, *wearing an army jacket. He is propped up by a single crutch and points an air rifle at* SYLVIE.

Is that loaded?

SONNY JIM: Give you two guesses.

SYLVIE: No?

SONNY JIM: What's your second guess?

SYLVIE: Perhaps you could point it away…

SONNY JIM: Is it making you nervous, missus?

SYLVIE: Can you put it down please, James?

He lines up the rifle.

SONNY JIM: 'In a world shot to hell, one man will stand alone to fight for freedom… In the land that time forgot, a hero will rise… In a city under siege, where was justice…? Right here.'

He makes the sound of a pump-action shotgun and 'fires'. He then plays the victim, complete with slow motion and gruesome effects of the bullet's impact. He falls to his knees, arms to the heavens.

'No! It's payback time.'

He makes the sound of machine-gun fire as he mows down the enemy. He stops as he feels SYLVIE's *gaze.*

I don't understand why more people aren't interested in war.

SYLVIE: It doesn't take many.

She gently takes the rifle and puts it down.

I hope you don't mind me calling by, James.

SONNY JIM: My friends call me Sonny Jim.

SYLVIE: I never see you with your friends.

SONNY JIM: I keep to myself. Work on my models. Got a whole squadron hanging from the ceiling in my room.

SYLVIE: Did you serve?

SONNY JIM: Honourable discharge. Best years of my life. Taught me how to survive. You know the trouble with you civilians? You're not simpatico with your surroundings. No awareness. Numb. Can't sense danger. [*He looks out.*] Look at all these backyards full of dogs doing what their owners should be capable of doing themselves.

SYLVIE: So why do you own a dog?

SONNY JIM: For the company. [*Calling*] At ease, Soldier! As you were! [*He salutes.*] I'm teaching him how to salute. He can put his paw up like this. [*He demonstrates.*] Soldier's an attack dog. Highly trained. He wouldn't lock his jaw on someone unless I gave a direct order. Loves children.

SYLVIE: He sounds delightful.

SONNY JIM: Everyone forgets that dogs are just people too.

SYLVIE: Why were you discharged, Sonny Jim? Was it your leg? Were you shot?

SONNY JIM: The dog bit me. Look, missus, I'll save you having to ask. I don't have anything further to offer regarding your loss. I don't fraternise with minors so I didn't know her.

SYLVIE: Don't... diminish her.

SONNY JIM: She may have had a little crush on me. The uniform has that effect. Hence, I was aware of her presence prior to... well...

SYLVIE: You can say it.

SONNY JIM: Her abduction.

SYLVIE: Is that what you think happened?

SONNY JIM: I don't want to upset you.

SYLVIE: I'm beyond that.

SONNY JIM: It does no good to say it.

SYLVIE: Say it.

SONNY JIM: Rape. Murder. Maybe not even in that order. I couldn't live with myself if I was the father.

SYLVIE: He couldn't protect her. That's hard for a man. And men don't speak, so... Detective Holloway told him to check under the house at night. Said runaways often hide there to be close. To hear how much their parents miss them. We told him that Ruby didn't run away. But Ray checks anyway. He looks down there every night with a torch.

SONNY JIM: I see him every day, your husband.

SYLVIE: He sees you walking your dog on his way to and from work.

SONNY JIM: 'Work'? Is that what he tells you? Missus, he rides the train all day. And when he's not on the train I see him in the window at number twelve.

SYLVIE: Grandma Moon's?

SONNY JIM: Little wonder he won't sell.

SYLVIE: You're mistaken. He's at work.

SONNY JIM: Up and down the line. Looking out the window for a little girl in a ruby-red dress covered in full moons. Does your husband carry a weapon?

SYLVIE *shakes her head.*

He should have a weapon. Needs to place himself inside the mind of the enemy. How does he think? What are his patterns? Routines? Needs? Wants? Weaknesses? I would make him my personal mission. I would hunt him down like a dog. I would cut his genitals off and feed them to him slowly because these people are animals!

SYLVIE: [*looking out*] It's ruined your mother's washing.

SONNY JIM: Oh no, I won't hear the end of that. She's always on Soldier's case. Not a pet person. Keeps threatening to have him put down. I'd like to have her put down.

SYLVIE: I'm sure she means well.

SONNY JIM: She doesn't.

SYLVIE: Is she often out this late?

SONNY JIM: She's out of town. Nagging a relative.

SYLVIE: Do you want me to bring that washing in?

SONNY JIM: She'll do it.

SYLVIE: When's she due back?

SONNY JIM: Why all these questions?

SYLVIE: I'm sorry.

SONNY JIM *takes out a little notebook.*

SONNY JIM: Can I read you something?

She nods. He sits.

It's called… Actually it's better when I stand.

He stands and clears his throat.

It's called 'Mother'…
[*Reading*] 'Shut up
Stop talking to me
Leave me alone
Will you
Get out of my room
I'm not in your womb
Anymore…
Shut up
Shut up
Shut up
Shut up! Shut up! Shut up!
… I love you.'

He closes the book. Silence.

It's not published.

SYLVIE: It's…

SONNY JIM: It's a poem.

SYLVIE: I thought it might be.

SONNY JIM: I've never read that to anyone. I tend not to have visitors. Apart from the police. When your little one disappeared. We hit it off in many ways. Like-minded, I suppose.

SYLVIE: You and Ruby?

SONNY JIM: The police. They appreciated my ability to handle the situation. I'm familiar with the concept of the street canvas. Most people fall apart. I had the presence of mind to offer them refreshments. Walking the street for clues and witnesses, as they were, I knew they would need to be provisioned. I inquired about their firearms. They informed me they carried a thirty-eight snub-nosed Colt. One of them had a Glock nine-millimetre, which I thought was interesting. They asked if I'd seen anything. I told them everything because often details that don't seem to be important can be, such as vehicles that have come and gone.

He shows her a page in his notebook.

I generally keep a log of unfamiliar cars in the street. Number plates. Make and model. It's a hobby of mine.

SYLVIE: Do you often lose your temper, Sonny Jim? Is that why Soldier attacked you?

SONNY JIM: He didn't attack me. I'm his master. He's highly trained.

SYLVIE: Maybe Ruby aggravated him that day…?

SONNY JIM: He never touched her.

SYLVIE: Do you ever walk him by the church in the dead of night?

He picks up his rifle.

SONNY JIM: What's she been saying about me?

SYLVIE: Veronica?

SONNY JIM: The old witch in number three. Always complaining about Soldier 'soiling holy ground'. I know what this is about. On the evening in question, he was sniffing around the church, clawing at the soil. I thought he was going to dig up that priest who took off. As it happens, it was a grave. But a small one. For a tiny body wrapped in a black garbage bag. Wearing a ruby-red dress with full moons…

SYLVIE: Please, no…

SONNY JIM: It was a doll. So you tell whoever was spying through their curtain that Sonny Jim did not bury your little girl in the church. Check with Detective Holloway. I was in my room the whole time. My mother confirmed it. I was working on my model of a B52, one to forty-eight scale. Which remains to this day incomplete.

SYLVIE: Why didn't you report this?

SONNY JIM: Because I knew how it would look.

SYLVIE: If you didn't bury Ruby Doll then who did?

SONNY JIM: It's a mystery, missus.

SYLVIE: Are you sending her to us in pieces, Sonny Jim?

SONNY JIM: I would ask the one who gave her the doll.

SYLVIE: Do you know?

SONNY JIM: Who would you trust with your child?

SYLVIE: The babysitter?

SONNY JIM: Bad things happen in houses like that.

SCENE SEVEN

SYLVIE *is skipping with a rope.*

SYLVIE: [*chanting*] 'My mother told me
  That she would buy me
  A rubber dolly
  If I was good, good, good
  And when I told her
  I kissed a soldier
  She would not buy me
  A rubber dolly…'

  RAY *appears.*

RAY: Sylvie! Sylvie, you'll disturb the neighbours!

  She stops and breathes heavily, recovering.

SYLVIE: Too late, Ray. They're already disturbed.

RAY: I'm afraid you've lost me.

SYLVIE: Don't say that. [*She drops the rope.*] We have to dig up the church.

RAY: Isn't it enough that we just don't attend?

SYLVIE: Who knows what else is buried there. Is that her perfume on you?

RAY: What did Sonny Jim have to say for himself?

SYLVIE: He'd never admit it but he's not coping with his mother away. The sooner she comes home the better.

RAY: She passed away. You knew that.

SYLVIE: Did I?

Silence.

Somebody buried Ruby Doll. But she's gone again.

RAY: And now they're sending her to us. Piece by piece.

SYLVIE: They're trying to break us. Someone has our answer, Ray. We have to keep going. The further down this street we go, the closer we get.

RAY: But it's a dead-end street.

He embraces her, clutching her to him.

What are we doing? What are we doing to ourselves?

SYLVIE: We deserve this. We weren't there when she needed us.

She breaks away.

RAY: I can't keep this up, Sylvie. I can't sit down for dinner every night with a place set for her at the table.

SYLVIE: There will always be a place set. There is no family without her. If we miss her enough, we can resurrect her.

RAY: What if she's still alive…?

SYLVIE: We don't know that. [*She suddenly stops still.*] Ray…?

RAY: What is it, baby?

SYLVIE: When did this arrive?

RAY: What?

She points behind the armchair and fetches the large brown paper package hidden there.

I didn't even know it was there.

SYLVIE: Then how did it get in?

RAY *shrugs. A sudden ominous knock on the door echoes.*

[*Calling*] Go away! Leave us alone!

They stare at the package.

RAY: It's bigger than the others.

SYLVIE: Someone's been in here.

RAY: What if he found the key under the mat?

SYLVIE: Look at it. It's big enough for…

RAY: Don't say it, Sylvie. Don't even think it.

SYLVIE: Someone's been in our home, Ray.

RAY: We could move. We could sell the house.

SYLVIE: How would she know where to find us?

RAY: We could try again…

SYLVIE: We had a child, Ray. And we lost her.

RAY: And we searched for her. Over fences. Under bushes. Down drains.

SYLVIE: We failed her.

RAY: We covered poles and walls with her face.

SYLVIE: They kept covering her with lost cats and dogs.

RAY: We had a skywriter write her name across the sky, Sylvie. There isn't any more that we can do.

SYLVIE: We can find her.

> RAY *suddenly goes to the package.*

Don't open it!

> *He lifts the lid and stares in at the contents.*

Show me.

RAY: Don't let it upset you.

> *He holds up a doll torso with one arm.* SYLVIE *laughs and takes it from him.*

SYLVIE: Don't you see? We can start putting her back together. Where are the other pieces? Give me the rest of baby girl.

> *She attaches the other doll's arm and two legs.*

He can't hurt us… [*Looking out*] Ray…? Where's Ruby?

RAY: I don't know, Sylvie! I don't know!

SYLVIE: The mannequin! She's not under the street lamp. Somebody's taken her. Who could be that cruel?

RAY: Maybe it's a sign, baby.

SYLVIE: They want me to lose her all over again.

RAY: Maybe it's time we put this to bed.

SYLVIE: It has to be him, Ray.

RAY: Who?

SYLVIE: The wizard. He's the one doing this to us.

RAY: We mustn't jump to conclusions.

SYLVIE: There has to be an end.

RAY: I'll look out for Mr Gallows on my way to number seven.

SYLVIE: Yes, the babysitter. She has to know something.

RAY: Don't open the door for anyone.

> SYLVIE *nods.*

Do I get a kiss?

> *She doesn't move. He leaves. She curls up in the armchair and winds the key on a music box. She opens the lid and a lullaby plays as the tiny ballerina pirouettes. The street lamp shines but there is no Ruby mannequin.*

SCENE EIGHT

A solitary spotlight on RAY. *He walks on the spot to the sounds of the night: a distant barking dog, the faint echo of a hymn being played on an organ in the church and a window shutter flapping in the wind. He stops still. The sound of a foreboding foghorn doorbell.*

RAY: [*calling*] Dawn…? Dawn…?

> DAWN *appears. She wears an old and frayed oversized jumper, a beanie and has flesh-coloured rubber bands strapped across her face, making her look deformed.*

DAWN: Been expecting you. Saw you go into the other houses. Knew I was next.

RAY: Do you know why I'm here, Dawn?

DAWN: Something about Ruby. It's always about Ruby.

RAY: It's colder in here than it is outside.

DAWN: Wouldn't know. Don't go out anymore.

RAY: Is there no heating?

DAWN: Too big. Too many cracks for the wind to whistle through. Can you hear it?

> *She whistles like the wind.*

RAY: What's that smell?

DAWN: It's the rubber.

RAY: From what?

DAWN: Do you want to know a secret, Mr Moon?

> RAY *nods. She drags a large, old suitcase towards him.*

You should prepare yourself. Going to be a bit of a shock when I open it. And you have to promise not to tell my parents. They don't know. Do you promise? You have to swear.

RAY: Open the suitcase, Dawn.

> DAWN *opens the suitcase.* RAY *stares into it.*

DAWN: Hello, you. Who are you looking at? Hmm? With your big blue eyes... And cute little pigtails... Do you want to come out to play? Come to Mummy...

> *She takes out a doll. It is a miniature Ruby.*

That's my girl... She's a little shy. Isn't she just perfect?

> RAY *picks out similar dolls from inside the suitcase.*

The others weren't right. Can see where I went wrong now. Have to learn from the mistakes.

RAY: Who are all these for?

DAWN: Only make them for me. Could never sell them. They're my babies.

RAY: You make them?

DAWN: Down in the basement. Down in my 'dungeon'.

RAY: So you gave her the doll?

DAWN: I was being nice. Is that a crime?

RAY: Did you bury her doll in the church?

DAWN: I don't like these questions.

RAY: Dawn, have you been sending those packages?

DAWN: What packages?

RAY: Don't play games with me.

DAWN: I don't even go out anymore. [*She brushes the doll's hair.*] I miss babysitting for you. Like stepping into the page of a picture book. Behind the little red door in the little white house. Where I had Ruby all to myself. Tuck her in. Read her stories. Brush her hair. Such beautiful hair. Not like my old pile of rope.

RAY: What have you got on your face, Dawn? Are they rubber bands?

DAWN: Don't come any closer please.

RAY: They must be hurting.

DAWN: I'm used to them.

RAY: What are you doing to yourself?

DAWN: 'God made the seas
   God made the lakes
   God made Dawn
   Well, we all make mistakes.'
   Only thing I ever learned at school was how to hold myself in
   contempt. Nobody can hate me more than I do.
RAY: Take them off, Dawn. For me? Please.

   She slowly removes the rubber bands.

   That's the girl… There, you look lovely…

   She breaks into a shy smile.

DAWN: I do not. [*She stares at the doll.*] Look at her pretty little pixie
   nose. That's how I'll have mine done. Have my teeth bleached too.
   First, the surgery. The facial fractures will help the diet because you
   can't chew food. Have to move away. Change my hair. Change my
   name. 'Rose'. Need to lodge the form. Work in fashion. Already make
   my own doll's outfits. And Rose is the perfect name for a label. My
   friends would call me 'Rosie'. I've practised my signature. It has a
   heart for the dot above the 'i'.
RAY: What's wrong with 'Dawn'?
DAWN: It's plain and it won't do!

   Silence.

RAY: Ruby's middle name was Rose…
DAWN: Your little princess broke one of my dolls once. Snapped its head
   off for no good reason.
RAY: Not our Ruby. She was a good girl.
DAWN: Quite a temper. Real mean streak.
RAY: Did you get angry at her, Dawn?
DAWN: Don't call me that.
RAY: Somebody's sending us Ruby Doll parts in brown paper packages.
DAWN: Have you put all the pieces together?
RAY: It's tearing my wife apart…
DAWN: Your house needs a grief chimney too. For the sorrow. We just
   kept breathing it in, plumes of black smoke, all these years. Nowhere
   for it to go.
RAY: Where are your parents? Are they upstairs?
DAWN: Can't go up there. They don't receive visitors. [*She rings a little
   bell.*] That's their bell. They'll think I'm down here talking to myself.
   [*She rings the bell again.*] You're going to get me in trouble. [*Calling*]

I'm coming! [*She whispers in his ear.*] I used to have a favourite doll. Every day I dressed her. Brushed her hair. Kissed her goodnight. But Daddy said it was time to 'grow up'. One day dolly was gone. Never did find her.

RAY: Dawn, when you say 'doll' do you mean Ruby?

A train's horn sounds in the distance like a ghost.

DAWN: The last train's calling. One day I'll get on that train and never come back.

RAY: Is Ruby somewhere in this house, Dawn?

DAWN *slams the suitcase closed.*

DAWN: [*singing*] 'She's not in the room
She's not outside…'

RAY: Do you know where she is?

DAWN: [*singing*] 'Hide from the world
The curtain girl…'

RAY: Dawn, where do you think our Ruby is?

She removes the red dress with white dots from the doll.

DAWN: You'll never know what I'm thinking. I can make myself think stranger thoughts. Keep everyone from knowing what's inside my head. Have to have my thoughts for myself.

RAY: It's you sending the packages, isn't it? Admit it, Dawn, you're not well.

DAWN: The packages come from number six!

RAY: You've seen Professor Ogle with the packages?

DAWN: He goes in and out with them all the time. Up to no good in there. Not me. I don't even go outside.

The train's horn sounds closer, bearing down, passing and then fading. She listens intently.

The trouble is I'm not a real person yet. But I'm going to become one.

The sound of distant thunder and falling rain.

Hear that…? They said we should expect rain… I don't need to be told to expect rain… It's raining inside, Mr Moon. It's raining inside me.

She hands the doll's dress to RAY. The thunder rumbles.

SCENE NINE

The sound of an answering machine message.

DETECTIVE: [*voice-over*] Ray, Sylvie, it's Detective Holloway. Would you give me a call at the station as soon as you get this message?

The sound of a final beep. SYLVIE *stares at* RAY.

SYLVIE: Did you hear that?

RAY: What, baby?

SYLVIE: The message on the machine.

RAY: When?

SYLVIE: Just then. Detective Holloway. You didn't hear that just now?

RAY: You're imagining things.

SYLVIE: They must have found her, Ray. He told us to call.

RAY: Sylvie, they don't make those kinds of calls. They come to your door. Look at the machine.

SYLVIE *looks at the answering machine.*

It's not flashing… She's not coming home.

SYLVIE: Don't say that. Why can't she just walk in through the front door? Why can't it end like that?

Silence.

What did Dawn have to say for herself?

RAY: I shouldn't need to tell you.

SYLVIE: Please?

RAY *hands her the doll's dress.*

RAY: She admits she gave Ruby the doll. But Dawn doesn't leave the house now. So she can't be delivering the packages. She pointed the finger at the professor.

SYLVIE: He never had anything to do with Ruby.

RAY: Except when he had that panic attack out front. Remember he collapsed? And Ruby took him a glass of water?

SYLVIE: Such a good girl…

RAY: And Professor Ogle just shuffled away like a wounded beast. Couldn't even look at her. Next day she found the glass on our doorstep with a red rose floating on water… What was a grown man doing giving a red rose to a little girl?

SYLVIE: What does he do in that house?
RAY: I heard he's an inventor.
SYLVIE: Of what?
RAY: It's a secret.

SYLVIE *dresses the headless doll.*

SYLVIE: Where do you go each day, Ray?
RAY: To work.
SYLVIE: So when I call you there tomorrow, what will they say?
RAY: Don't call me there.
SYLVIE: I could come with you…
RAY: You can't come in to work, Sylvie.
SYLVIE: On the train. I could look for her with you.
RAY: I don't know what you're talking about.
SYLVIE: Every day you desert me, Ray. Condemn me to these walls. To this silence broken only by the barking of Sonny Jim's dog or the ringing of the school bell or the wizard's knocking at the door. And all the while you're hiding in your mother's house and riding the lines to escape me.
RAY: It's not about you. Not everything's about you.

Silence.

SYLVIE: Why didn't you buy Ruby an ice-cream?
RAY: What has that got to do with—?
SYLVIE: You didn't know she was going to Grandma Moon's. Why wouldn't you have bought an ice-cream home for her?
RAY: I just assumed she…
SYLVIE: You saw her skip by, didn't you? The last time you saw her. Down Flaming Tree Grove. You watched from the window.
RAY: What window?
SYLVIE: Veronica's window. You didn't call me from the train station. You waited in there precisely eleven minutes before emerging from the lane and you stopped the ice-cream van on its way back up the street because you thought, 'Why not treat myself?'
RAY: Where is this coming from?
SYLVIE: Don't think I don't see you slip out for your nightly rendezvous. Cheap promise in your step. Climbing over the fence to her boudoir like a teenage boy. Into her powdery skin and painted lips.

RAY *reaches for her. She turns away.*

Don't touch. Try your tramp at number five.
RAY: Don't be like this. Baby...?

She allows him to caress her.

SYLVIE: Is this what you do to her in there?

Suddenly he violently clutches her hair.

Ray, you're hurting me...
RAY: Tell me to stop.
SYLVIE: What if I don't want you to?
RAY: Oh, I'm not going to stop. But I want you to tell me to. Plead with
     me. Beseech me to stop. And I'll just keep going.
SYLVIE: Stop... please stop...
RAY: Beg me!
SYLVIE: Please, I beg you! I don't want to do this! Please... stop.

They stare. He releases her.

RAY: She's gone, Sylvie. Long gone.
SYLVIE: No, Ray. We're close. Closer than ever. [*She looks out.*] They're
     cracking. Don't you see? They want to be caught.

SCENE TEN

A solitary spotlight on SYLVIE. *The sound of a creaking tree, a wind
chime and a street sign clanking in the wind. She huddles against the
cold as she watches* CARL *inside his house, packing a suitcase. He is a
dishevelled man wearing a fawn lab coat. The sound of a door buzzer.*

CARL: [*calling*] I'm nearly ready!

SYLVIE *appears.*

SYLVIE: Going somewhere, Professor?
CARL: They're coming for me. I want to be sure I'm all packed before
     they arrive. [*He closes his suitcase.*] Are they waiting out there?
SYLVIE: Who?
CARL: Dear lady, I am so sorry. [*He starts to weep but pulls himself
     together.*] I want you to know I believe in the law. The Law of Physics.
     Motion. The Universe. It's my purpose to know these laws. To apply
     them. And yes, even defy them to reach into the unknown. I knew

this day was coming… Knowledge has always been my comfort, you see. But never the knowing of this.

SYLVIE: The knowing of what, Professor?

CARL: Can you hear them?

Silence.

Is that the sirens…?

SYLVIE: Professor?

CARL: Carl. Call me Carl. I'm not qualified.

SYLVIE: Carl, I'm here about Ruby.

CARL: I know why you're here. What can I say? I'm a failure. She's gone. With the others. They're all gone. I killed them all.

Silence.

SYLVIE: What others? Carl?

CARL: [*producing a folded document*] It's all in my statement. Typed and signed.

SYLVIE: You're confessing…?

CARL: Yes.

SYLVIE: Just like that…?

CARL: I can't harbour it any longer.

SYLVIE *suddenly lashes out at him. He absorbs her blows. She stops. He looks out.*

The stars seem further away tonight. Don't you think? I fell for my wife as soon as she said her name… 'Celeste'. Always was compelled by the heavens. The cosmos. The great beyond. Beneath my blanket of darkness pierced by brilliant dying lights.

SYLVIE: Can I see that?

He hands her the document. She unfolds it and reads.

CARL: It may not be chronological. I can't be certain of the order initially. Deductive reasoning tells me Penelope was first. Then Ruby. Then… Well, you can see the names for yourself. What have I done…?

SYLVIE: Where is she?

CARL: That's the problem. Where are any of them? I've racked my brain, believe me.

SYLVIE: This is full of names. What sort of monster are you?

CARL: What happened was in the pursuit of science. The furthering of mankind. Every experiment comes at a cost. It's the price of progress.

SYLVIE: Tell me what you did to my little girl.

CARL: She loved cartoons. Used to come over after school to watch them on our television. One day I was troubled by my work and found myself beside her watching this duck or rabbit or mouse, I don't recall the species, but it was being chased by a pig or a wolf or a cat. When suddenly, and quite implausibly I might add, the prey produced a circular black object and laid said object in the path of its predator who proceeded to drop down the hole, disappearing into thin air. Interesting idea, I thought. Sadly, one posited by this cartoon without any scientific calculations to support what, in astrophysical terms, was a revolutionary concept. And parents let their children watch these programs.

SYLVIE: I want to hear you say it.

CARL: You want to know how I did it?

> *She nods.*

'Professor Ogle's Portable Black Hole'. My wife made that same face when I told her. I thought Celeste would understand my invention, being a travel agent. She sends them to the four corners of the Earth and I send them into a vacuum in space entirely void of matter.

> *He fetches a brown paper package.*

SYLVIE: Where did you get that package?

CARL: Dear lady, the package is not relevant. [*He puts on protective gloves.*] It's what's inside. Of course, as soon as the complications occurred I reverted to this smaller prototype to ensure no further human interaction with the black hole. I've gone through seventy-four mice trying to get your Ruby back.

SYLVIE: Back from where?

> *He lifts the lid and very delicately removes a small, round, black object and lays it on the floor.*

CARL: Sceptics say it's just a circular piece of two-dimensional black rubber. But, you know, ask the mice. Don't get too close. It could suck you right in.

SYLVIE: Carl, what did you do to Ruby?

CARL: Strictly, I didn't do anything. But I take full responsibility for my invention. My theory is I must have left the lab door unlocked, allowing Penelope to creep in. She was always hungry for mice.

She'd already eaten three. Ruby must have followed her in and stumbled upon my first prototype. Much larger diameter. Very powerful. Would have taken them both in an instant.

SYLVIE: 'Penelope' is your… cat?

CARL: Was. And I came back from the pet shop where I'd been purchasing more mice to discover that the house was empty.

SYLVIE *suppresses a smile.*

SYLVIE: And did you have names for these mice, Carl?

CARL: They're all listed… Minnie, Audrey, Alice… All the mice are in sequential order as I was able to refer to my notes. [*He fetches a clear plastic cylindrical tube with a rose inside.*] This is the Astro-Transporter I used. Fits four mice per mission. Without the rose.

SYLVIE *stifles her laughter.*

It's important for the mice to have companionship. [*He regards the black hole.*] Seems I underestimated the black hole. The sheer force of it. The hunger. It consumes all who come into contact and I'm powerless to stop it. Everyone seems to disappear… It's the nature of the Universe. [*He tries to control his emotions.*] I'll miss this house… my laboratory… my stars…

SYLVIE: [*reading the document*] Did you name one of the mice Celeste?

CARL: No… she's gone too.

SYLVIE: Gone where?

CARL: Out there. The black hole took my beautiful wife.

SYLVIE: But my husband said he saw Celeste just the other day. She's still running her travel agency two doors down from the bookstore.

CARL: Dear lady, that's impossible. She disappeared off the face of the Earth. I haven't heard a peep from her. Believe me, I've tried every calculation to bring her back. Ruby too. Every formula. Every law. Every proof. I know the equation, Mrs Moon, but I just can't solve it.

Silence. He removes his gloves, picks up his suitcase and looks out.

One last look up before they take me away… They should be turning down the grove any minute. You'd think we could hear the sirens by now… That's strange…

SYLVIE: What is?

CARL: She's not under the street lamp.

SYLVIE: Somebody took her. Again.

CARL: It's the black hole. It's ravenous. [*He listens.*] There they are.

> *He listens with relief to the sound of distant police sirens.*

Can you hear them…? Here come the sirens…

> *Blackout. The sirens pass and fade.*

EPILOGUE

RAY *stands in the moonlight streaming through the window.*

RAY: [*calling*] Sylvie…?!

> *He picks up the headless doll and notices a drawstring on its back. He pulls the cord and Ruby's creepy voice plays. Her ghostly whisper reverberates like a secret.*

RUBY: [*voice-over*] It begins like a fairytale…

> *He pulls the drawstring again.*

[*Voice-over*] … but how does it end?

> *A slow knock at the door echoes.*

RAY: [*calling*] Go away! Leave us alone!

> *The naïve refrain on the wooden pipe echoes.* RAY *pushes aside the armchair and kneels down. He opens a trap door in the floor and shines a torch into the darkness.*

[*Calling*] Ruby…? Ruby, are you down there…? It's Daddy… Don't be afraid… You can come out now if you like, baby.

> *Silence. He closes the trap door.*

'Where's Ruby…?'

> *He searches the room.*

'Where can she be hiding?'

> *He looks behind the curtain to reveal the Ruby mannequin.*

'There she is!'

> *He takes out the mannequin, lifts it up and spins around. Another slow knock at the door echoes. He puts the mannequin down.*

[*Calling*] I said go away! You can't come in!

SYLVIE *appears, dressed as Ruby. She is carrying a brown paper package.*

SYLVIE: [*as Ruby*] Daddy…?

RAY: What are you doing?

SYLVIE: [*as Ruby*] It's me. Aren't you happy to see me?

RAY: Of course! Look at you… Hello, baby girl…

SYLVIE: [*as Ruby*] The wizard let me in.

RAY: There is no wizard, baby.

SYLVIE: [*as Ruby*] I'm sleepy.

RAY: You're home now. I'll tuck you in.

SYLVIE: [*as Ruby*] Did you miss me, Daddy?

RAY: Your mother and I have been sick with worry.

SYLVIE *points to the doll.*

SYLVIE: [*as Ruby*] Ruby Doll lost her head.

RAY: Look in the package, baby.

SYLVIE *lifts the lid and takes out a doll's head.* RAY *attaches it to the doll.*

There. All back together again.

SYLVIE: [*as Ruby*] She's been sad.

RAY: I know.

SYLVIE: [*as Ruby*] Hold me.

He embraces her like a child.

[*As Ruby*] Hold me tighter, Daddy. Squeeze the life out of me.

RAY: I've got you.

She kisses him passionately on the lips. He responds, then pulls away.

No! Don't, baby!

She stares at him.

SYLVIE: This is how it goes, doesn't it?

RAY: No…

SYLVIE: Put your hands on me.

She kisses and claws at him. He responds, then pulls away.

RAY: Stop!

SYLVIE: [*as Ruby*] Why didn't you bring me home an ice-cream?!

RAY: Go to your room!

Silence. She looks at the mannequin.

SYLVIE: I've worked it out, Ray.

RAY: What?

SYLVIE: Grandma Moon wasn't calling to ask where Ruby was. She knew exactly where Ruby was. She was in her kitchen. Dead.

RAY: Why do you want to hurt me?

SYLVIE: An accident, of course. Forgetful as she was, the dear old thing. What was it this time? Disinfectant in her iced tea? She couldn't read the labels. Easy mistake for the old woman to make. And you answering the phone telling her to wait until you got there. 'Mother's distraught about Ruby,' you told me, 'I'll go calm her down.' And you drove off down the street. I remember thinking that was strange. By the time you got the car out of the garage you could have run. But you knew you needed to put something in the boot when you got there.

RAY: Will you listen to yourself?

SYLVIE: And so you drove, past the flame trees, blackened by the night, and reversed into her driveway at the end of the cul-de-sac. Through the back door to see Ruby lying on the floor in a pool of blood and vomit. Not moving. Not breathing. No pulse. Grandma Moon fussing about in the pantry, trying to read the labels, her frantic falsetto ringing in your ears… 'What have I done? What have I done?'

RAY: Stop this right now.

SYLVIE: And you sent her for a bucket and a mop while you rolled your little girl up into a big, black, garbage bag, with the drawstring pulled tight. You turned off the outside light. You were thinking of everything. After closing the boot of the car you put your mother to bed. With extra pills to see her off to sleep, the other side of which she'd wake up without memory. Senility suddenly her ally. You could depend on it. Then you called me from her phone before cleaning the floor and running home. I was too distracted to notice that you'd left with the car and returned without it.

RAY: I decided to door-knock on the way back. In case anyone had seen anything.

SYLVIE: Nothing to see. You'd thought of everything. When you collected the car the next day where did you dump the garbage bag?

RAY: There was no garbage bag!

SYLVIE: What did you wrap her up in? A rug? A bedspread?

RAY: There was no body! She never arrived!

SYLVIE: You thought you got away with it. That I would never even think it, let alone work it out.

RAY: You want to play this game, Sylvie? Who's to say you weren't the last one to see her? Apart from a few highly unreliable witnesses? What if Ruby never even set off for Grandma Moon's because you'd already—?

SYLVIE: What? Say it.

RAY: Why was there no dinner on the table? What was it that you were so busy doing?

SYLVIE: I told you. Dulcie came in here in a state about her missing parrot.

RAY: There is no parrot! She made it up! You made it up!

SYLVIE: That's not how this goes, Ray!

RAY: Hell, you made her up!

SYLVIE: Don't you dare pull it all down!

RAY: Dulcie Doily is nothing more than the sum total of every pious, judgmental thought you've ever had!

SYLVIE: [covering her ears] I won't hear this!

He fetches the birdcage, tears off the cloth cover and dumps it on the floor between them. It is empty.

RAY: The game's over, Sylvie.

SYLVIE: [singing as Dulcie] 'Kum bah yah, my Lord…' [She claps to the tune.] 'Kum bah yah…'

RAY: She's just a lonely old spinster who takes refuge in the church. And look what you've turned her into.

Silence. They sit, desolate.

SYLVIE: The woman is a witch. It's a far more accurate rendering than your hollow incarnations.

RAY: 'Hollow'? [As Sonny Jim] 'In a world shot to hell, one man will stand alone to fight for freedom.'

SYLVIE: You and your crippled manhood.

RAY: You and your pickled prima donna.

SYLVIE: [singing as Veronica] 'The crying bed
Take back those words unsaid…'

RAY: [as Veronica, mocking] 'What do you say, Ray? Once more with feeling?'

SYLVIE: [as Sid, mocking] 'Um, um, um… people don't like clowns anymore.' [As herself] People don't like weak fools.

RAY: I'm not the one shovelling painkillers down my throat.

SYLVIE: Only to escape your gallery of madmen. [*As Carl*] 'Dear lady, it's the black hole. It's ravenous.'

RAY: [*as Dawn*] 'God made the seas
God made the lakes
God made me
Well, we all make mistakes.'

They laugh a little then stop, broken. Silence.

SYLVIE: Was there a child, Ray? Was there ever once actually a little girl?

RAY: Don't, Sylvie. That's too far.

SYLVIE: But what about the Gallows boy? We made him up.

RAY: We had to.

SYLVIE: Was she really taken from us, Ray?

RAY: You know she was.

SYLVIE: Or are we just having the same nightmare?

RAY: But we can't sleep.

SYLVIE: Tell me what we know, Ray. It helps when you tell me what we know.

RAY: [*breaking down*] We know that once upon a time there was a little girl called Ruby Moon.

SYLVIE: Past tense.

RAY: We know that she set off to visit her grandma at the end of the street but she never arrived.

SYLVIE: Our prized Ruby. Our gem.

RAY: We can't keep doing this every night. We can't keep riding into this tunnel.

SYLVIE: This is our train.

RAY: We're facing the wrong way, Sylvie. We can only look back. And nothing lies ahead because all we can see is what's already passed.

SYLVIE: But we can see the light. It's back where we came from.

RAY: We can't keep blaming ourselves. Or even those around us.

SYLVIE: Then who? Who?!

She weeps. He pulls himself together for her.

RAY: What if… what if it was a stranger?

SYLVIE: Do you know?

RAY: It's so obvious…

SYLVIE: Tell me.

RAY: Who else could it be…?
SYLVIE: Ray…?
RAY: We told her to never trust a stranger…
SYLVIE: Which stranger? Who? You tell me who!

She clutches at him. He hums the 'Greensleeves' tune.

But haven't we thought of him before?
RAY: I remember now. When I bought the ice-cream I saw the signed photo of Veronica stuck up on the inside wall of the van.

SYLVIE *hums 'Greensleeves'.*

SYLVIE: Da da da da, da-da da da da…

He hums with her. She smiles.

Yes… it must be him! We should call Detective Holloway!
RAY: We will, baby. First thing in the morning.

He offers her pills and a glass of water.

Try and get some sleep. The sun will be up soon.
SYLVIE: My head will be clearer tomorrow…

She takes a pill. This time she swallows it.

Ray…? Maybe it was the telephone repairman…?
RAY: Yes, baby. Maybe it was.
SYLVIE: Or the wizard? Do you think it was the wizard?
RAY: You never know.
SYLVIE: We'll get him tomorrow night.
RAY: Of course we will.
SYLVIE: I still don't trust the others.
RAY: I know.

The telephone rings. They stare at it.

Are you going to get that?
SYLVIE: You can hear it ringing?

He nods. They stare at the telephone. She moves to answer it. Just as her hand reaches for the receiver the phone stops ringing.

Do you think it was her?

RAY *opens the worn leather book at the last page.*

RAY: [*reading*] 'Flaming Tree Grove was stilled like a painting
Black birds on the wire on the verge of fainting

As the horizon burned and the flames licked higher
A little angel disappeared down the corridor of fire.'
SYLVIE: Don't let it end like that, Ray...

> RAY *closes the book. The sound of the naïve piano refrain echoes.*

It can't end like that...

> *The full moon shines blood-red with increasing intensity. The naïve piano refrain reverberates with a shy Ruby singing.*

RUBY: [*singing, voice-over*] 'She's not in the room
She's not outside
Hide from the world
The curtain girl...
Behind the curtain girl.'

> *The lights slowly fade to leave the parents silhouetted by the blood-red moon with the rocking horse rocking slowly back and forth and the Ruby mannequin standing sentinel. Blackout.*

THE END

www.ingramcontent.com/pod-product-compliance
Lightning Source LLC
Chambersburg PA
CBHW041934090426

42744CB00017B/2052